'Fifteen Thousand Hours' : A Discussion

'Fifteen Thousand Hours'
Secondary Schools and their Effect on Children

A Discussion

Barbara Tizard, Tony Burgess, Hazel Francis,
Harvey Goldstein, Michael Young, Jenny Hewison
and Ian Plewis

with a Response from the Authors

University of London Institute of Education

First published in 1980 by the University of London Institute of Education,
20 Bedford Way, London WC1H 0AL.

Printed in Great Britain by Reprographic Services,
University of London Institute of Education.

Note on Contributors

University of London Institute of Education

Barbara Tizard is Reader in Education in the Thomas Coram Research Unit.

Tony Burgess is Lecturer in the Teaching of English.

Hazel Francis is Professor of Educational Psychology.

Harvey Goldstein is Professor of Statistical Methods.

Michael Young is Senior Lecturer in the Sociology of Education.

Jenny Hewison is Research Officer in the Thomas Coram Research Unit.

Ian Plewis is Research Officer in the Thomas Coram Research Unit and the Department of Statistics and Computing.

Institute of Psychiatry, University of London

Michael Rutter is Professor of Child Psychiatry.

Barbara Maughan, Peter Mortimore, Janet Ouston and **Alan Smith** are Research Officers.

Contents

Preamble

These papers were presented to an Institute of Education staff seminar, held in June 1979. The idea behind the seminar was not to make a concerted attack on what the group thought was a bad piece of research. On the contrary, it was because *Fifteen Thousand Hours** reported a major project, of both theoretical and practical significance, that it seemed important to discuss it.

The nature of research in the social sciences is widely misunderstood: there is a tendency for the publication of a research report to be swiftly followed by attempts to disseminate its findings, and where possible to apply them, often in a wholesale fashion. Specific reforms are advocated on the basis of research findings as though they were certain to be successful. When this proves not to be the case, another policy reversal may occur, and a general disenchantment with research and researchers sets in.

One way to try to forestall these difficulties is by ensuring that extensive critical discussion of major research reports takes place, examining the assumptions of the researchers, the questions they set out to answer, the appropriateness of their methods, and the validity of their conclusions. Such discussions should not only help to prevent over-hasty administrative action, but also help to formulate the nature of further investigations or interventions which the research findings point to. We hope, then, that having read these papers, the reader will not shrug his shoulders and conclude that 'nothing has been proved'. Our aim was rather to clarify what the Rutter study did and did not establish, and to stimulate discussion about the problems involved in evaluating secondary schools.

Barbara Tizard
Thomas Coram Research Unit,
41, Brunswick Square, London WC1N 1AZ.
April 1980

---

* **Rutter, M. et al** (1979), *Fifteen Thousand Hours.* London: Open Books.

What Makes an Effective School?
Tony Burgess

Educational research surprisingly seldom achieves what is publicly expected
of it: to settle difficult questions with evidence. The compelling feature of
Fifteen Thousand Hours is its appearance of having hit this gold. An impres-
sive base of data supports an architecture in which many common sense per-
ceptions about schools are co-ordinated. This professionalism makes the
more important a critical engagement with the detailed story, with what the
book has to say about schools and about which parts in the process of
schooling need to be scrutinized and understood. The general thesis is
exciting: schools matter. But the detailed message is, I believe, profoundly
wrong and one which could end by diverting attention from questions which
we should be asking about inner-city schools.

The world of this research, the inner-city school, is one which has been
treated for a decade or more according to a tradition, common to teachers,
teacher trainers and researchers, which has been fundamentally curricular in
its concentration. My comments on this research derive from such a perspective, affected by working with young teachers training specifically for inner-
city areas and by an interest in the linguistic and language-linked questions
raised by the interaction of school, public expectations and local, multi-
cultural communities. What should schools do? What should they be
teaching? How are teaching and learning to be set going, in authentic ways,
within a divided culture, hostile over all to the achievements and history of
working-class people? Curricular in concentration, such a tradition interro-
gates schooling, above all, about the content and values which it seeks to
realize.

By contrast, the focus of *Fifteen Thousand Hours* is almost exclusively
managerial. From a teacher's perspective, concerned with realizing quality
of teaching and learning, there are immediate oddities. How, in the present
context of debate, can a research have taken success in public examinations
as the single, measured outcome of academic achievement? How can there
have been no attention to the aims of classroom teachers, to innovative

practice and curriculum and to the effect of physical conditions, dismissed as insignificant, in facilitating or constraining practice? The book omits discussion of curriculum and pedagogy, along with the necessarily evaluative stance which such discussion would entail, and seeks, instead, to limit attention to the effectiveness of school as a managed institution in meeting a range of demands which are by common agreement asked of it. This is to omit the core of school's teaching and learning enterprise, and, moreover, to risk an uncritical view of conflicting pressures and expectations placed upon it. In the present political climate, it is a strategy, which, I believe, could well have dangerous consequences. ·

Fifteen Thousand Hours is constituted in appearance as a critique, on the one hand, of doubts about limits to what schools can achieve, on the other, of tolerated differences of 'process variables' between schools. It will be hard to read the list of process variables, which are actually discriminated, as other than conventional 'inefficiencies'. The possibility which the research raises, above all for energetic and innovative head teachers, is that a well-managed school, given proper attention to the cultivation of a positive, rewarding, reinforcing ethos, can make a decisive difference to the life chances of children in inner-city areas. But this of course is no critique at all. The recipe is for more of the same, advanced without considering whether a more radical examination of what schools are actually doing is needed.

In support of this direction teachers are finally offered no more than the conventional wisdom of social psychology by way of moving forward. The familiar ring of the concluding chapter is good as far as it goes: teachers' expectations about the pupils' work and behaviour, the models provided by the teachers' own conduct, the feedback that the children receive on what is acceptable performance at the school, positive rewards, managed pupil acceptance of school norms, pupil positions of responsibility, shared activities between staff and pupils. But we have been there before on other occasions — and in the book we surely get to be there twice. The discriminated set of process variables, supposedly established independently of research bias, reflect on inspection precisely this array of social psychological prescriptions. Critique and guidance are unmistakably circular, each revealing a fundamentally conservative and managerial concentration.

Doubts about the effectiveness of inner-city schools have not, I believe, been ultimately those which are addressed and treated within the scope of this research. The final sentence of the book is disarming and modest: 'We may conclude that the results convey the strong implication that schools can do much to foster good behaviour and attainments and that, even in a disadvantaged area, schools can be a force for good.' But the question confronting those who work at the most concentrated point of inequality in British society has not been whether schools may do some good, some more than others, but whether they can be a force for substantial change, and, if so, how.

The pessimistic case about schools, which this book seeks to disarm, has at least the merit of posing a clear question for teachers and others concerned with the education of working-class children. That question has challenged the limits of school's effective social power, as presently constituted, in meeting the systematic reproduction of inequalities in society more widely. The thesis of *Fifteen Thousand Hours* leaves ambiguous and disguised whether the possibility of substantial inroads into such reproduction of inequality is being claimed for schools on the basis of the research's findings, or merely that some can do a little better than others within the leeway allotted them. And better in what terms? For those who have taken the questions raised by inner-city schools to be those of values and curriculum, the omission of such considerations stands as a further ambiguity.

Nevertheless, the task which *Fifteen Thousand Hours* proposes for research is a challenging and important one, in which the methodological experience of the authors is valuable. My concern, so far, has been with the more detailed message, with the isolation of discussion of schools' aims from their ordering and managing as institutions. My fear has been that managerial goals are being offered as a substitute for more fundamental debate about curriculum and pedagogy. I close with some more methodologically oriented comments.

My central reservation is whether the normal methods of psychology, measured correlations of variables abstracted from the school process, will ever of themselves answer the question: What is it that makes an effective school? This is not a denial of some role for measurement. But the heart of the matter, for me, is in the intricacy and argument of prior, conceptual analysis. What I miss in the approach of *Fifteen Thousand Hours* is, above all, two things: one of them a sense of history, both a broad and more local framework within which the achievement of these schools can be placed and evaluated; the other a sense of actual texture of the schools themselves.

The history which we are looking at in this research is one, after all, in which the education system, looked at one way, has made massive gains for working-class children staying into sixth forms and taking public examinations, yet, from another vantage, has failed to shift the alliance between independent schools, Oxbridge and commanding positions of power in the economy. Can we seriously pose questions about schooling or schools without considered, historical analysis of the questions which we are posing?

Secondly, texture. The method of this research, generating from school sets of variables of general applicability, leaves unexamined the specific siting of different variables within individual schools. May not that specificity — what happens, the ways in which these variables interact within different schools — be a critical issue? Indeed, may not study of specific interactions be a crucial check on the significance of more general process items? The instinct of many teachers is to begin to answer the question 'What is it that makes a good school?' a great deal more informally by locating themselves in a school they think good, hoping to pick up the tone, the feel of it, the subtle ways in which process is mediated. Should not research seek for ways to align itself with that? A range of such studies would have to argue their way through values, beliefs, significance, history. They would not have immediate generalizability, but they might in the end be truer than an approach which runs the danger of delivering the parts of the machine but not the enterprise itself. The signal contribution of *Fifteen Thousand Hours,* to conclude positively a critical response, is that it has raised and made urgent such questions.

A Question of Method
Hazel Francis

This book[1] poses some rather general questions, and then sets about an attempt to answer one of them. The general questions are: Are schools important? Do they make a difference to pupils' lives? What sort of difference? How do they make this difference? Now these are very general indeed, and include the major question of what kind of difference schools might make over and above what would happen to children if they weren't at school at all. The authors, however, do not wish to attack this question, and settle for the more limited and manageable question of whether differences between schools are related to differences in the outcome for pupils. Within this question the outcomes of interest are predetermined. They are: attendance at school, behaviour in school, academic attainment, and delinquency. These are aspects of pupil behaviour *in* school, and their relation to what happens *after* school is not at all clear. In other words the book is not attempting to say how differences between schools may affect pupils' lives later. The selection of a limited number of aspects of behaviour in schools also means that the authors can say nothing about other features of pupil behaviour. It is important to remember this, lest any factors which are thought not to affect the selected behaviours should be too readily dismissed as not affecting pupil life at all. This is particularly true of factors which the authors describe as ecological variables, matters such as the size of the school, type of building, type of management, social balance of intake, and sex composition. (It is also quite possible that a different sample of schools than the twelve inner London secondary schools used in the study would yield a different picture.) The factors which the authors do find in their study to be related to the outcomes for pupils are described as process variables. These are much more to do with the way teaching is carried out in the school than with the background measures to which I have just referred. We now have a picture of the more limited question the authors attempt to answer, namely whether differences in the ecological variables, or in the process variables, as described above, affect the selected behaviours of pupils in twelve inner

London secondary schools. The problem I am going to develop in relation to this is how best to set about answering the question.

The authors have chosen to use a well-established correlational model of research, controlling the initial variation in pupils as far as possible, exploring the ecological and the process variables, and then analysing the relationships between these and the outcome measures. Because the study has a longitudinal aspect, the authors also lean a little towards attempting a causal explanation. In other words they not only claim a correlation between process variables and the selected outcomes, they also suggest the processes lead to the outcomes. Now it seems to me that this is a limited model, which in the last analysis gives very little information. In the present state of knowledge about schools and their effects on pupils even this little is very welcome, but it does raise the question of whether, in the future, it will still do.

One reason why I think it won't do is that the relationships between the selected ecological and process variables and pupil outcomes are not those obtaining between independent and dependent variables. Pupil behaviour is part of the processes of school life, and both depend on the physical and social context. The authors of *Fifteen Thousand Hours* comment on the interactive nature of processes in schools, but they still treat them as causal. Yet the processes influence pupils, and pupils influence the processes, from the very first day in school. Two groups of children in the same school and with the same teachers can show very different interaction patterns in the teaching and learning situation. The picture is similar for different intakes in the same school, and for different intakes in different schools. Within any group something of a spiralling effect is likely to occur, as the contributing individuals firm up their behaviours in characteristic ways, so the group processes of teaching and learning become more clearly defined, and they in turn further constrain the pupil's behaviour. I have seen something of this spiralling effect in the case of young children learning to read. The child's increasing ability to read alters the interactive process of teaching and learning. Success breeds more success, while inability breeds helplessness. I am suggesting that in an educational context a model which relates processes to pupil outcomes in a causal manner is too limited, and that a model which elaborates on the interactive nature of pupil and teacher behaviours may be more revealing and more useful.

But an interactive model rather than a correlational model, may still be mechanistic. It, too, can fail to catch the pupil as a human agent. The authors of the study appear to be aware of this problem, to the extent that they speak of the pupils as participating in the initiation and maintenance of processes. An important point follows this observation. Pupils' behaviours must be related to motivations and intentions arising out of personal histories, as well as to other features of the contexts of learning. That pupils initiate and maintain processes in school raises a question about the initial differences between pupils in the study. Differences in intellectual ability were controlled for to some extent. It is possible, however, that the pupils were bringing with them social and academic expectations of schools and of themselves that they had acquired in their primary schooling. In other words, they were bringing into their secondary schools behaviours which had already been learned elsewhere in relation to school processes, and which would help form the characteristic processes of their new schools. Secondary school processes, in other words, are not static characteristics of the schools, but are in part formed by the pupils engaged in them, who may well have brought shades of their primary schools with them.

The discussion so far has not referred to the ecological variables mentioned by the authors. In the inner London study they did not seem to have an important effect on pupil behaviours in the schools. Nevertheless, this may not be the case in the country at large, and some extension of the interaction model is needed to accommodate them. I suspect that in order to achieve this, one might do worse than explore what has come to be known as general systems theory.[2]   Here an important distinction is made between open and closed systems. The mechanistic correlational model is well suited to the structure of closed systems, but not to those of the open type. Thinking about the latter has been much influenced by the biological sciences, and by notions of differentiation and development within a system, and maintenance of it from without. An organism can be seen as having an internal environment for processes of differentiation and development to take place, and an external environment where ecological variables form the life support system for the organism. I wonder whether this isn't a rather useful metaphor for the school.

If we were to think of a school community as a living organism within its sustaining environment, we could define the sustaining environment variables. In other words, we would have to say what counted as life supporting in a relevant sense, and in this connection some of the ecological variables introduced in the *Fifteen Thousand Hours* study would certainly count. We might see the type and state of the schools as being similar to a habitat; we would see the material resources, the parent provision, the teaching ability of the staff, and the pupils' own abilities brought into the picture as resources or food supplies to the system. It is interesting in this connection that some aspect of either teacher or pupil may well be seen as an ecological variable, while another aspect perhaps will be seen as a process variable within the school system. It is a curious analysis in that it cuts across persons as entities. This may well be novel in our thinking about schooling, but it may be useful, and may not present an insurmountable difficulty. If we are able to clarify what would count as the supporting environment, and the associated ecological variables, we can then turn to an account of the school system. If we are taking the metaphor further we shall have to consider what would count as differentiating cells and developing organs within the body of the school, and also what would count as developmental processes. In this case the pupils might be seen as discrete individual cells combining in functional substructures, such as informal pupil groups or formal groupings in the school, these themselves being organs or parts of organs of the body. Teachers would similarly be individual cells, with different functions, and taking their place within an appropriate organ model. I find the metaphor challenging, though considerable mental labour will obviously be involved in elaborating it. Hopefully, the end product would not simply be a list of process variables applicable to a school, but a characterization of important units within it, their functioning relationship, and the processes developing within them.

I think an important problem in this thinking is to differentiate between the life of the school and the life of the individual pupil. Quite clearly they have different conceptual status, and it may be that two different system models need to be developed if questions are to be asked about both. Nevertheless, it is just possible that a suitable analysis of the school life of the child might well rest within an analysis of the life of the school. If such a framework could be developed, then observation and measurement of appropriate variables would help to characterize the relative importance of different parts of the system and the rates of differentiation and development within it, and help answer the question of how what is going on in the school is related to the behaviours of individuals pupils. The relevant mathematical model or models for data analysis would probably include the mathematics of rates of change in multi-dimensional space, not that of sampling distributions.

Anyone who has had much to do with schools will realize that a picture which suggests smooth development and smooth change is not quite true. Sometimes things can quite clearly and suddenly come adrift in a school, or can change dramatically in a more positive sense. When this is the case it may be that a different mathematical model from the kind of mathematics behind correlation theory or smooth rates of change is required to characterize the situation. Recent development of catastrophe theory[3] suggests that this might be helpful. Here we have a notion that one of the variables in a situation may increase to a point where others quite suddenly shift onto a different plane. An example might be that the size of class could be steadily increased within a school without any obvious sudden consequence, though increases in stress of various kinds might be noted. At some point, however, the increase might result, not in a further small increment of stress, but rather in a very sudden collapse of discipline. No doubt other examples could be brought to mind very readily by teachers and administrators. Differences between schools, or differences within a school from one time to another, might well be looked at with this kind of model in mind. It does not replace any of the other models so far considered, but it does add another tool for the analysis of what goes on in schools.

The discussion so far has been based on the analysis of pupil behaviours within a developing social system. A fuller understanding of what goes on in schools must also call on an analysis of the meanings of these behaviours and of what the schooling experience means to the child. This realm, the realm of social and personal meanings might be handled by an anthropological approach. The problem would be to find what elements in the picture had what sort of meanings for the participants. It seems likely that these elements would be related to the structures analysed in the system approach to the life of the school. It would be a very difficult task to sort out the nature and structure of these relationships, but to achieve it would be to build a most fruitful psychology of education.

Fifteen Thousand Hours poses some very important questions. The authors set out to answer a specific question in a limited well-defined way. The methodology used is now a familiar one in educational psychology, the measurement of a number of variables in a situation, followed by analysis of their intercorrelations. But it takes no account of the nature of the situation in which these variables are identified and measured. The general questions posed in *Fifteen Thousand Hours* expose this underlying problem, but the specific question that is answered ignores it. If I ask any pupil in a secondary school what it is about the school that affects attendance I can get a list of suggestions. A list from one child went like this: 'boring lessons, not teaching very much in the lesson, endless note-taking (we avoid this because if you know it's only going to be notes you can skive off, and know that you can pick them up from somebody else), poor lesson preparation, poor supervision of registration, leaving registration to one of the pupils.' I didn't ask the child to complete a list, it seemed to me there was enough already. These were the kind of process variables listed in *Fifteen Thousand Hours* – not precisely the same ones, but certainly the same kind. We can get lists of process variables from almost anybody involved in schooling. But what we really want to know is how these and the many others that we could think of, together with the ecological variables we could identify, are interrelated for a particular child, or for many, in a complex real-life fifteen thousand hours story.

Notes

1. **Rutter, M. et al.** (1979) *Fifteen Thousand Hours.* London: Open Books.
2. Useful references are:
   Beishon, J. and **Peters, G.** (1976) *Systems Behaviour.* 2nd Edition. London: Harper and Row.
   von Bertalanffy, L. (1968) *General System Theory.* Harmondsworth: Penguin.
3. An interesting reference is: **Zeeman, E.C.** (1977) *Catastrophe Theory.* Reading, Mass. Addison-Wesley.

The Statistical Procedures
Harvey Goldstein

Introduction

Few educational research studies are so entirely free from methodological weaknesses that a sufficiently determined and diligent critic cannot find enough material with which to mount a plausible attack. The measure of a good critique, however, is not its achievement in exposing all the weaknesses of a study, but its illumination of those weaknesses which really matter. It will be useful to expand a little on this topic before discussing the present study.

Suppose it was discovered that the authors of a report had calculated a standard deviation incorrectly. At one extreme this error might be so serious that its correction would also involve the reversal of several important conclusions. Clearly, such an error should be publicized so that unjustified inferences are not drawn. If, however, the error were not so serious and if the replacement of the incorrect by the correct value were to change nothing of substance, we might take one of two views. We could recognize that mistakes will always occur, satisfy ourselves that this was not a serious one and say nothing more. Alternatively, we might feel that the authors of the report should have been more careful, and we might then wish to treat the mistake as evidence contributing to an existing opinion of serious incompetence. Examples of both types of response can readily be found, and each has some legitimacy. There is a third type of response which takes whatever errors of such kind as can be detected and uses them in an attempt to undermine the credibility of a study, even though the sum total of the errors could not be said seriously to threaten any conclusions.

Having made the above distinctions, the real difficulty is to recognize them in practice. In particular, it is extremely important to distinguish minor blemishes from major and potentially catastrophic ones. A failure to do this has often lead to a debate losing its audience, who either cannot follow its detail or do not feel that there would be profit in doing so. As in all good criticism, the point is to evaluate the importance of any defects and then to communicate their essence to the intended audience in terms which are intelligible. I shall attempt to do this in the following comments, bearing in mind that the typical reader will not be a practising statistician. I should also emphasize that this review is concerned with the statistical and design methodology of the study and not directly with such matters as the choice of measures, etc.

A brief outline of the study

A 'cohort' of approximately 2,000 children were followed from before their entry to secondary school until their first public examinations. For these children, who attended twelve inner London secondary schools, there were 'outcome' measurements of attendance, delinquency, behaviour and examination results and the basic analyses compared average values for the twelve schools. One set of analyses then studied the extent to which differences between schools could be accounted for by various characteristics of the school, after making allowance for possibly differential intakes at eleven years. A second set of analyses, this time using the school rather than the child as the unit of analysis, also looked at the way in which various characteristics of the schools were associated with the outcome measures.

Adjusting for intake differences

The authors rightly point out that causal inferences from survey data concerning 'outcome' differences between schools, are greatly strengthened if appropriate adjustments can be made for pre-existing differences between the intakes to the schools. Thus, comparatively good examination results at sixteen might simply reflect an academically selective intake at eleven and if it were possible to 'equate' such intake factors between schools, and if the outcome differences are little changed by this, then we would feel more justified in attributing these differences to other measured factors. The principal difficulty with this approach lies in ensuring that we have been able to measure *all* the relevant intake factors. Rutter *et al.* use, principally, verbal reasoning score and occupation group prior to intake, justifying these on the grounds that they were the best predictors of the outcome variables. Previous research, however, has shown that there are many other variables — family size, subject attainments, etc. — which are also at least as good predictors, and also associated with selective intake to schools. It is curious that the authors do not even discuss the possibility that the variables they use may only make a partial adjustment, and it remains an open question as to how much of the subsequent differences between schools could be attributed to additional variables not used. This seems to be a substantial criticism in view of previous research and implies extra caution in interpreting the results of the study. An incidental technical point here is that it is the *within-school* correlation of intake variables with outcome which it is appropriate to study and not the over-all one used by the authors.

If we turn to one of the statistical analyses which uses the intake adjustment procedure, we discover some technical inadequacies which seem to cast further doubt upon some of the conclusions and which also seem to contribute to a general picture of a less than fully competent technical expertise. Table 5.9 in Appendix G reports an analysis of variance which shows that verbal reasoning (VR) score accounts for 28.6 per cent of the variance in the outcome examination score and that there are significant remaining differences between the schools after adjusting for VR. The obvious next question is how much of these school differences can be accounted for by, say, the 'process' or 'physical' or 'ecological' factors measured during the study. This is done in another analysis given on page 171 in Table 9.4. Here, however, VR score only accounts for 14.5 per cent of the variance (thus performing a less adequate adjustment), and indeed the total variance is only 25.9 per cent, and this includes that taken up by parental occupation, process score, etc. Needless to say, in this analysis, the process and other factors had significant effects after adjusting for VR and occupation. There arises the question of whether, given the full adjustment of which VR is capable as in Table 5.9, the process score, etc., would still be related to outcome. The authors, however, seem unaware of the relationship between the analyses in 5.9 and 9.4, and the fact that they could easily have used VR in 9.4 in just the way it is used in 5.9. (It would, incidentally, be more informative if we could be given the sizes of the differences between schools etc., rather than just the percentage of variance accounted for.) Admittedly, the authors do mention that there are some technical problems associated with using linear models (analysis of variance and regression analysis) but these are not as insurmountable as they seem to suggest. Instead, they prefer to introduce 'log linear' models which utilize the outcome measures in terms of 'percentage of good attenders', 'good exam results', etc., rather than 'mean attendance score'. 'mean exam score', etc. The log linear models, however, suffer from many of the deficiencies already mentioned and some more serious ones. For example, the adjustment for VR uses VR group in only three categories as opposed to seven for the previous analyses, with half the children falling into the middle group. In this respect it is an even more inadequate adjustment than before. While, in many ways, these log linear model analyses are the most interesting in the book, they actually do not carry as much useful information as the previous analyses might have done had they been better executed. There is also a technical deficiency in the presentation of the results of these log linear analyses, in that the G^2 statistic cannot really be considered a useful 'measure of importance' since it depends on the sample design and its components cannot sensibly be interpreted separately (page 169).

There are other deficiencies involved with the execution and interpretation of the analysis involving intake adjustment, but the above should indicate that much is left to be desired and they do not encourage the reader to place a great deal of confidence in the authors' results.

School ethos

Some of the most widely publicized findings of this study concern the so called 'school ethos' factors. The authors define 'ethos' in terms of thirty-nine 'process' variables. These are chosen out of a larger number of forty-six on the basis of having statistically significant correlations with at least one outcome variable. It is not very surprising that using a composite score based on these thirty-nine variables they found high correlations with examination score and behaviour. By choosing the significant and hence larger correlations only they are capitalizing on chance; and by choosing a large number to go into a composite score they are virtually guaranteeing reasonably high correlations, especially with a sample size of only twelve schools (on which more below). It is not difficult to obtain similar results with purely random data (Preece, 1979). There is no real attempt to provide a definition of school ethos which has an educational basis and the authors do not seem to appreciate the need to provide one. In what claims to be a major educational report this seems an important oversight.

Units of analysis and sample size

As explained earlier, some of the analyses in this book (such as that in Table 5.9) use individual children as units of the analyses, whereas others use the school. The trouble with the latter (more numerous) analyses is that the sample size is only twelve. Apart from the fact that these schools are not really a random sample so that an inference to any other population of schools is problematical, the authors place far too great a reliance on the results of significant tests, by tending to dismiss non-significant relationships as unimportant. A striking example occurs on page 99 where local authority schools have an average ranking on attendance which is twice that of voluntary aided schools and where boys' schools have an average rank twice that of girls' schools for behaviour and examination results. Such differences are very large but, not surprisingly, they are non-significant since the sample size is only twelve. At the bottom of the page the authors conclude that the sex differences are of negligible importance. Not only is that conclusion unjustified, but it results from a fairly elementary statistical misunderstanding and diverts the authors from further consideration of factors which have an obvious potential for explaining school differences.

Conclusions

The above comments have been almost entirely negative so that it will not be surprising if I conclude that the study results should be treated with caution if not scepticism. Nevertheless, the basic *idea* behind the study is a useful one and there is here some prima facie evidence that genuine school differences may exist which are related to measurable school factors. Undoubtedly, there should be further research along these lines which avoids the deficiencies of the present study. As for educational practice, it would seem wise to hesitate before applying any of the results of this study too literally, and the quite strong conclusions drawn by the authors in Chapter 10 need to be viewed rather cautiously.

Reference:

Preece, P.F.W. (1979) 'Fifteen Taus and Rhos.' *Brit. Educ. Research Assn. Newsletter,* August 1979.

A Review
Barbara Tizard

I think that *Fifteen Thousand Hours* is a very important and, I hope, seminal book. Major British educational research projects are pitifully scarce. The strengths of this one are that, as one would expect from the Rutter stable, it was meticulously planned and executed: a lot was known about the children before they entered secondary school, so that it is in a sense a longitudinal study; systematic observations were made within the school, and related to other measures; and the authors addressed themselves to very significant questions. Their first message — that the characteristics of a school power-fully affect the behaviour and achievements of its pupils — should bring comfort to any teacher beset by self-doubt. True, *qua* parents, all of us know this to be true. But, *qua* teachers or social scientists, we tend to be more influenced by the evidence of the effect of social class and IQ on school performance. 'Hard' evidence that within a social class and IQ group schools *do* count is therefore heartening.

It should, perhaps, be pointed out that some doubt must remain about the extent to which the study does in fact establish that differences in the children's achievements reflected school rather than family influences. Although the authors have statistically equated the schools for fathers' occupation and children's school records at age ten, other possibly important family characteristics were not taken into account. For example, some working-class parents with children of average ability are more knowledgeable about and interested in education than others. If these families select a secondary school with a 'good' reputation, and thereafter give their children more educational support, the children's school career will depend to a greater extent than the authors allow on parental as well as school character-istics.

That said, the study certainly shows that children of the same social class and similar test scores at age ten fare very differently in different secondary schools. The authors' choice of 'outcome' variables (public examination results, orderly classroom behaviour, truancy and delinquency rates) reflects the aspirations of most parents. Whatever our social class or race, we usually hope our children will get O-levels, and keep out of trouble with the school authority and the police.

Nevertheless, these 'outcomes' are by any standards limited: no school, surely, would state as its *aims* that the children should get a few O-levels, and keep out of trouble. Wouldn't most teachers and parents want to add, at the least, such aspirations as that the child should enjoy school, learn to relate tolerantly and co-operatively to other children, be helped to feel good about herself, feel able to tackle the difficulties and problems she meets, develop wide interests, and so on? And shouldn't we be able to state academic aims for the 30 per cent of children who are not going to get any O-levels or CSE passes?

Still, the authors can hardly be blamed for not addressing these issues, when there is so much general confusion about them. On the one hand, some heads act as though they were running grammar schools, and stake their reputation on the number of O- and A-levels the school clocks up. On the other hand, radical teachers who argue that the function of schools is to validate and perpetuate the class sytem find it difficult to articulate positive aims for the school. What *are* secondary schools aiming at? And how are we to assess their success?

The authors' second, and more important, message is that differences between schools in children's achievements and behaviour can be shown to be related to differences in school and classroom characteristics. Again, this message is of a practical interest to us as parents: when we come to select a secondary school we should like to be able to identify the characteristics of the school which will meet our child's needs. For educationalists and social scientists, an attempt to measure the processes within the school which result in particular outcomes is of considerable importance.

As the authors freely admit their 'process variables' were a very rum collection of forty-six items. They ranged from whether the children's work was displayed on the wall (related to examination successes and delinquency rates, but not to classroom behaviour or truancy) to the number of the teacher's disciplinary interventions (related to classroom behaviour but not to examination success).

In a thought-provoking discussion, the authors conclude that these items were, in fact, measuring aspects of the school's 'ethos'. This concept brings us back to the consideration of what the expectations are within the school for both teachers and children, and by what mechanisms these expectations are transmitted. That the measures chosen are crude, and the mechanisms mostly guesses, is undeniable. What matters is that the authors *did* succeed in measuring aspects of school life often thought to be unmeasurable, and that the study *does* address itself to the crucial question of how a school's functioning affects children. It is to be hoped that it will provoke further studies in this area. (A small caveat: nowhere do the authors present a list of the data about each school. The importance of preserving anonymity is clear, but one or two identifying variables could have been omitted — e.g. size of school, voluntary or maintained status — and the readers would still have been able to assess and re-analyse much of the data for themselves.)

A Case Study of the
Limitations of Policy Research
Michael Young

It was not my brief in this paper to summarize the book under examination; however, I found it useful in working out my reactions to the study by Rutter and his colleagues, to try and construct an over-all picture of the model of research with which they were working, and the aspects of the problems that they thought important. This seemed particularly relevant in light of their statement on page 107 that:

> the study was not designed to test any particular theory about schooling, nor was our analysis based on any pre-conceived ideas about which particular aspects of school process should be important.

Though there is a recognized tradition in the social sciences of claiming not to have 'any pre-conceived ideas', this claim is always shown in practice to be untenable. For Rutter and his collegaues to mount this research at all, they had to have such ideas, in terms of which they entered the schools — ideas about what to look for or disregard, how and whether something could be quantified, what to take as evidence, how to decide what meaning to attach to events they observed, etc. These matters are given scant discussion in the book, and the diagram which follows (page 34 below) is an attempt to point to some of those that need to be questioned. As with any other piece of research, it is important not to separate any evaluation from the context of its production and reception. It was sponsored by the Inner London Education Authority, which though it has a distinguished record in public education, has in recent years come under some criticism, often ill-informed, of the standards of achievement in its secondary schools. It was supported by the Department of Education and Science, which since at least 1975, when it started funding the research, has been under political pressure to 'improve standards'. This sponsorship is consistent with the purposes of the research that were presented to the participating schools. They were told by Rutter and his co-researchers that they were seeking to 'identify the characteristics of a good school'. In other words, the idea that, in some sense, there was 'one·best way' that could be identified with some claims to objectivity, and which would provide the basis on which teachers in 'less successful' schools could model their activities, was already built in to the research before it started.

Fifteen Thousand Hours received widespread and favourable publicity quite beyond the attention given to most research reports. This took a variety of forms, but the sensationalized summaries in the popular press, brought to mind an earlier book from the same publishing house (Open Books), Neville Bennett's *Teaching Styles and Pupil Progress*, which whatever its author's intentions became seen as an authorative and factually based critique of a whole tradition of primary school teaching. There is some indication that *Fifteen Thousand Hours* is taking a similar role in relation to secondary schools. Without any formal enquiry I have come across a number of comprehensive schools in which the Headteacher has distributed summaries of the concluding chapter to the staff, and called a staff meeting to implement what the authors recognize as their more speculative comments, as points for action. This study has as far as I am aware received very little *critical* attention. The reasons for the welcome with which it has been received may be more that it adds 'scientific' confirmation to certain current prevailing opinions, and less on account of the strengths of its arguments and supporting data. It is for this reason that I see a critique of some of its assumptions as important; I shall restrict myself to examining four specific aspects of the book.

1. The model of research
In *Fifteen Thousand Hours* we have a study which divides the social world of the school into two kinds of relatively discrete sets of quantifiable variables. The dependent variables, or school outcomes, are those factors in the experience of pupils that are thought of as the outcome of going to school: attending (regularly or not), good behaviour (or bad), doing well (or badly) academically, and committing (or refraining from) acts reported to and identified by the police as delinquent. The independent variables the researchers divide into four kinds: ecological, physical and administrative, intake factors, and school processes, which are themselves sub-divided as I have shown in the diagram (page 34). The reader is asked to accept, without discussion, their divisions and their groupings, and we can learn very little from the book about how, and on what basis, they obtain indices or measures for their variables. Though no explicit theory of schooling is developed, the plausibility of the model of variable analysis as a basis for inferring *influence*

rests on a theory which at no stage do they examine. These assumptions are that the 'factors' that they abstract *do* represent, in some fruitful way, the reality of school and that they *are* interrelated as a system of interdependent parts. Perhaps this point can be made clearer if I indicate the kind of 'factors' which their model does not regard as important: questions of power, conflict, boundary maintenance, identity protection, classification and categorization (of pupils, teachers and knowledge), as well as the ways in which the social relations of the wider society might mediate processes within the school. Any research based on variable analysis depends entirely on quantified data and its interpretation. It follows that anything of significance will emerge through the process of quantification and the various tests of statistical significance. This raises a number of problems which can be illustrated from any part of the study. I will take one example – what they refer to as the 'behaviour component of school outcomes'. Pupil responses on a questionnaire are given a meaning in terms of the researchers' conception of good behaviour. So we have a picture of their 'well behaving pupils': they don't miss lessons, don't draw on the wall, wear uniform, are on time, don't engage in fights, don't wear anoraks, or chew gum, or comb hair in class, and do have a pencil. It is not that there is necessarily anything wrong with such a list, but rather that by denying significance given to the acts by the pupils, it actually precludes any understanding of *why* pupils act in such ways. Thus, built into the very model of research is a limitation on the guidance that might be given to teachers, who are unlikely to have the time to ask such questions. They claim that

> Because we were able to use measures of what was *actually* done in schools (including observations in the classroom) we were able to translate the previously noted variations in school climate and morale into the specifics of school practice. (page 180).

However, this just avoids the problem of *interpretation,* whether of classroom behaviour or questionnaire response.

2. The school as a social institution

This idea is a central theme of the book and is used to encapsulate what they call 'school processes'. Early in the book their concept of a social institution is clear:

> ... individual actions (are important for) the part they play in contributing to a broader school ethos. (page 55).

> ... our concern was ... with the sorts of actions which
> teachers and pupils could take to contribute towards the
> establishment of an ethos which would enable all those in
> the school to function well. (page 56)

The school as a social institution, therefore, means teachers and pupils accepting an agreed set of values, which enable the school to run smoothly. According to Rutter and his co-researchers, schools can be ranked according to the degree to which they comply with this ideal. This ranking is based on teacher responses to pre-coded questionnaires, though we are not given the schedules. Though there is a long literature of debate about the appropriateness of this value-consensus model of any institution, the point can be put simply in relation to schools. It neglects questions of careers and promotion, time-tabling, distribution of free periods, examination entries, competition for resources, etc., all of which become, in any school, issues of conflict and negotiation which cannot be considered if the assumption of value-consensus is given primacy. In another form, the model is re-introduced through the concept of ethos, which they suggest as accounting for the over-all association of school process variables and outcomes, though the unevenness of this association (39/146 items have correlations of 0.5 or more) make it difficult to know what sense to make of such an arbitrary summation. What is missing from the combination of the methods of variable analysis and the value-consensus theory of the school as a social institution is any sense of the reality, in how schools influence children, of the social relations between teachers and pupils, and the ways each attempt to understand the situations they face. Atomized responses and a presupposed consensus make it virtually impossible to relate the account the book offers to the actual experiences of schooling except in a narrowly prescriptive and legislative way.

3. The primacy of consistency

The points I have made about their value-consensus-model of the school as a social institution are linked to one of the strongest conclusions of their book, and one which was picked out in at least one daily newspaper. This is the emphasis on the importance of consistency and agreement among teachers and pupils. This is argued independently of what the teachers and pupils are being consistent about. Because they see the notion of the school as a social institution as important and because their model of a social institution is a value-consensus one, the claim is made that the school will be more effective if all agree. Thus, given the hierarchical structure of schools, such a prescription can give justification for head teachers to discipline dissident staff even when they may be emphasizing some of the positive proposals that the book itself makes. The recommendation, based on the authors' model not their empirical work, to give to consistency and coherence over-riding priority can only lend support to whatever philosophy, leadership or regime is dominant in a school at a particular time, regardless of the concrete values that a particular philosophy expresses. In a society that is deeply divided in terms of social class, sex and race it is inconceivable that such divisions will not be expressed and experienced as conflicts of interest within the schools. Prescriptions for consistency, backed up by statistical support as in this book, rather than a recognition and a willingness to work through real differences, can only lead one to plead that such conclusions and recommendations be treated with the greatest reservation by those in positions of administrative authority.

4. Other elements in school-society relations

Finally, a study which puts great emphasis on what teachers can do to improve school outcomes, and backs its claims with the legitimacy and objectivity of statistical analyses, necessarily de-emphasizes other elements in the complex totality of school-society relations. In *Fifteen Thousand Hours*, teachers are viewed, as they tend to see themselves, as being able to influence what goes on in the school and classroom, but as being able to do little about those matters which mediate society in the school. Not surprisingly, therefore, such matters take on a hazy and diffuse reality. Social-class relations are not mentioned, inequalities are expressed as differences in social background, the hierarchy of occupations in the division of labour is reduced to differences of ability and balance of intake, and totally neglected in terms of how it acts on the academic/non-academic divisions in the curriculum.

This book may be important for administrators and the senior management of schools, in playing down of the importance of certain factors – age of buildings, split sites, staff-pupil ratios, and indirectly in encouraging more centralized forms of administration. For the classroom teacher, and for pupils, it may be more important that they gain greater understanding of the powerful ways factors outside the school constrain their teaching and learning. However, to suggest something like that is tantamount to asking for a very different kind of study from *Fifteen Thousand Hours:* a study which would come up against much more difficult problems of funding and sponsorship, and would raise questions of accessibility to data, which never arose for Professor Rutter and his colleagues. Falling rolls, school closures, and cuts in resources are among the likely realities of secondary schooling in the next few years; in any attempts that groups of teachers and others, and, importantly, groups of schools make to combat the likely consequences, and to involve those outside education in resisting the predicted cuts in resources, *Fifteen Thousand Hours* is likely to be at best of marginal significance.

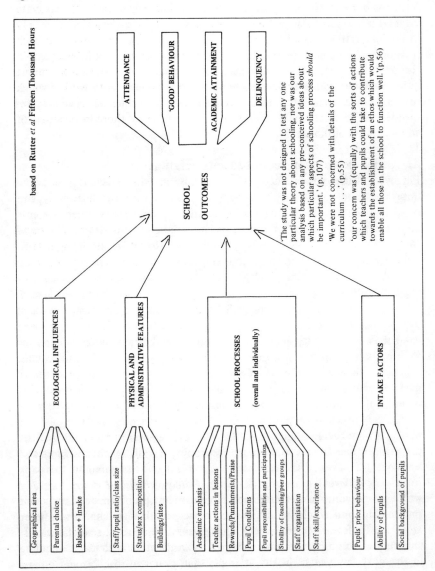

based on **Rutter** *et al* **Fifteen Thousand Hours**

ATTENDANCE

'GOOD' BEHAVIOUR

ACADEMIC ATTAINMENT

DELINQUENCY

SCHOOL OUTCOMES

'The study was not designed to test any one particular theory about schooling, nor was our analysis based on any pre-conceived ideas about which particular aspects of schooling process *should* be important.' (p.107)

'We were not concerned with details of the curriculum . . .' (p.55)

'our concern was (equally) with the sorts of actions which teachers and pupils could take to contribute towards the establishment of an ethos which would enable all those in the school to function well.'(p.56)

ECOLOGICAL INFLUENCES
- Geographical area
- Parental choice
- Balance + Intake

PHYSICAL AND ADMINISTRATIVE FEATURES
- Staff/pupil ratio/class size
- Status/sex composition
- Buildings/sites

SCHOOL PROCESSES (overall and individually)
- Academic emphasis
- Teacher actions in lessons
- Rewards/Punishments/Praise
- Pupil Conditions
- Pupil responsibilities and participation
- Stability of teaching/peer groups
- Staff organisation
- Staff skill/experience

INTAKE FACTORS
- Pupils' prior behaviour
- Ability of pupils
- Social background of pupils

Statistical and Educational Significance : A Comment
Jenny Hewison

Fifteen Thousand Hours is written and packaged in a style designed to attract the attention of 'all those professionally involved in teaching; and anyone with a care for the quality of education today' (publisher's description). Only a minority of such readers are likely to possess sufficient statistical expertise to appraise for themselves the data analysis procedures on which the book's conclusions are based: the remainder of the readership are reliant on the book's authors to present evidence and argument in a form they can understand. The criticism of the book expressed here is that its authors treat statistical and educational significance as synonymous terms, and leave the general reader with little option but to do the same.

To become specific: the existence of a statistically significant correlation between two variables is not in itself proof that the relationship described is educationally important. To judge the educational, or practical, significance of research findings of this kind, knowledge is required of the *magnitude* of the change in the supposed dependent variable (the 'outcome'), which might be expected to result from specified changes in the independent ('process') variables. By how much, for example, might attendance figures be expected to rise if schools improved their practices in accordance with the research findings? Or, at the extreme, if the 'process' score of the 'worst' school on these measures could somehow be raised to the level of the 'best', to what extent could this — even ideally — be expected to narrow the gap between the schools' levels of performance?

It is unfortunate that most of the data analyses presented in the book go no further than significance testing, i.e., they demonstrate the *existence* of relationships between certain variables, but are not addressed to the more practically informative task of parameter estimation.

When analyses are carried out on large samples, significance testing can be particularly misleading if used alone, because in these circumstances even very weak relationships between variables may be found to be statistically significant. To illustrate: in Chapter 9, which described the 'Composite analyses of all main variables', it is reported that, '... the "process" score of the school attended was correlated significantly with exam success even after taking all other variables into account'. At the end of the section in which this statistical analysis was reported (page 172), the authors state their interpretation of the findings: 'The conclusion is clear: children's levels of examination success are affected by the schools they attend, and the crucial features of schooling with respect to academic outcome include both school process and the balance of intake.' Such a statement may be misleading to non-technical readers, because the conclusion they are liable to draw from it is that process variables have been identified which play an important part in 'accounting for' outcome variation. This is not in fact the case: after other influences on examination performance have been taken into account, the size of the process effect is very small indeed (about 1 per cent of variance explained). Statistically speaking, this small effect is 'highly significant', but its educational importance is much less apparent. Influences on two other outcome measures, attendance and delinquency, are also analysed in Chapter 9, and the school process variables studied are reported to account for 0.75 per cent and 1.29 per cent of outcome variance respectively (the latter figure refers to boys only). Both of these contributions to prediction were found to be statistically significant at the .001 level, illustrating once again that great caution is necessary when assessing the importance of research findings in practical terms.

In Chapter 9, the authors do acknowledge that the process variables studied made only a small contribution to the prediction of attendance and delinquency, and that as yet unidentified variables must be playing an important role in the determination of between-schools differences. It seems likely, however, that the implications of this acknowledgement will not be fully appreciated by the general reader, not least because they run counter to the strongly positive impression created in the previous chapters. In Chapter 5, it is established that there are large differences between schools in the behaviour and performance of their pupils, and that these differences in outcome remain even after adjustment has been made for intake factors; in Chapter 7, schools are shown to differ on process variables, and schools' ranking from high to low process score is shown to be statistically related to their ranking on the adjusted outcome measures. The general reader may be tempted to put two-and-two together, and conclude that the process variables described in Chapter 7 are responsible for the between-schools differences in outcome shown in Chapter 5: strong words of caution would be required effectively to counter this tendency, and in these circumstances the technically-worded acknowledgements described above are unlikely to be sufficient.

It has been argued that caution is required when interpreting 'statistically significant' research findings: in the present case, further evidence would seem to be required in order to establish the educational significance of the school process variables identified. In this context, it is worth pointing out that if educational practitioners do endeavour to change their own school and classroom practices in the direction of improving their 'process score', then a large-scale natural experiment will have been set in motion. Monitoring of this experiment, and assessment of its outcomes, would be a most valuable contribution to the understanding of the mechanisms and issues involved.

Design and Analysis : A Comment
Ian Plewis

The authors of *Fifteen Thousand Hours* surely deserve our congratulations for their determination in collecting and analysing such rich data and for their success in achieving such a high level of co-operation with the schools in their study. However, I would like to suggest two ways — one relating to design, the other to analysis — in which the research could have been improved.

The circumstances of the study meant that, given limited resources, only a small number of schools could be observed. Hence it does not really matter that the schools were chosen by the researchers, instead of by a random selection, particularly as the total number of schools from which the sample was selected was also small (only twenty) and not particularly interesting in its composition. Whatever one thinks of the results, they would clearly be very much more valuable if they could be replicated in other different conditions, schools in rural areas, or Scotland, for instance. Without such replication, it is not possible to say how valid the conclusions are for schools in very different areas.

Although it is easy to be wise after the event, the authors might have been better advised to concentrate on a more homogeneous sample — perhaps mixed, medium sized, local authority schools — rather than try to achieve a mix of secondary schools. Some of the problems of interpretation which arise from the results on physical and administrative features of the schools given in Chapter 6 (and discussed by Harvey Goldstein) could then have been avoided.

Given that it is not possible randomly to allocate children to secondary schools (although, in passing, one might wonder whether the idea is as outrageous as it first seems) in order to relate differences in children's achievements to differences in school organization, it is crucial to try to eliminate intake differences between schools. The authors rightly give great emphasis to this. Nevertheless, there are three ways in which the control for intake was deficient. Firstly, the authors relied on just one or two variables to control for intake when others might have been appropriate; it should be remembered that the verbal reasoning score was obtained a year before the children actually started at secondary school. Secondly, some important interactions were found between input variables and school, i.e., the relationships between input and output were not the same for all schools. The authors chose to get round this by restricting their analysis to the middle VR band (50 per cent of the children) for attendance and examination results, but they did not discuss the fact that this restricts the generalizability of their findings. Thirdly, statistical adjustment for intake differences is bedevilled by measurement error in the input variables; it is difficult to know just how serious this might have been, but one would feel happier with the results if the problem had been considered.

Let me conclude by using the language of personal probabilities to evaluate the results of this study. This book has changed my views. From being indifferent about whether schools 'make a difference', I now feel about 65 per cent sure that they do. But a different design and a more complete analysis might have made that final probability much higher.

A Response to the Discussion Papers
Michael Rutter, Barbara Maughan, Peter Mortimore, Janet Ouston and Alan Smith

As Barbara Tizard emphasizes in her preamble to this set of papers, there is a most unfortunate tendency in the social sciences to react to research reports as if they existed in isolation. As a consequence, some pieces of research are unjustifiably dismissed because of methodological imperfections, whereas others are equally unjustifiably acted upon as if they provided the whole truth needed for policy decisions. All research is imperfect and no one study on its own ever settles policy questions (or even more narrowly defined scientific questions). Our investigation of secondary schools is no exception to that rule and hence we welcome this attempt to examine critically our findings and our conclusions in order to determine just what has and what has not been established. While we regret the rather negative tone of some of the critiques and the tendency to dismiss any piece of empirical educational research because it doesn't provide all the answers, some important issues are nevertheless raised. In this brief paper, we will not attempt to respond to each detailed point in the papers, but rather confine ourselves to comments on the major questions raised with respect to our research goals and strategies.

Aims and assumptions

Research goals
The conceptual approaches taken by the various authors differ considerably, and the papers serve to underline the point that there is no one 'best' way of tackling the varied questions involved in looking at school influences. Debates on educational questions can only benefit from consideration from a range of different perspectives, and we do not for one moment claim that ours was the only appropriate way of approaching the questions, and even less that this one study provides all the answers. Obviously it does not, even within the narrow framework of the goals we set ourselves. Even more obviously, there are many crucial educational questions which fell entirely

outside our field of enquiry. What we do claim, however, is that the study provides some relevant empirical data on one limited, but nevertheless very important, set of issues.

Thus, we started with the findings from earlier research which indicated school differences in various aspects of pupil progress. Our purpose was to determine whether these findings were an artefact of intake variations. If they were not, we hoped to identify which characteristics of the school might be important in constituting a potential influence on children's behaviour and attainments. This meant starting with the notion that it is sensible to consider schools as social units with definable characteristics. This is not to deny, however, that each teaching group within the school is also a social unit, with characteristics which are to some extent separate from those of the school as a whole. Indeed, other investigations have shown the importance of such class effects although it is perhaps pertinent to note that these have concerned primary schools, where children remain with the same teacher throughout, rather than secondary schools in which each child attends many different classes with many different teachers. In addition, of course, the experiences of each child within a single class are likely to vary, because children differ in their temperamental styles and in their backgrounds in ways which influence the nature of teacher-child interactions. These individual differences, like school class effects, are important and well worthy of study, but they were outside the scope of our own investigation. To obtain leverage on any particular issue it is always necessary to focus on a deliberately limited set of questions; that is the way of empirical research. It would be foolish and futile, as well as hopelessly grandiose, to try to solve all educational issues in one fell swoop. Our study neither does that nor claims to do that. Our response to the alternative strategies suggested by Hazel Francis and Michael Young is thus that, while interesting in their own right, they are applicable to questions which are different from those we set out to tackle in this particular piece of research.

Assumptions and preconceptions

Young suggests that our evaluation of schools was influenced by the fact that the research was funded by the Department of Education and Science and the Inner London Education Authority. In that connection, we should make it clear that neither body had any power to censor or alter our report, and that throughout the whole of the study there was no pressure of any kind for us to focus on particular aspects of school life, or to adopt any particular interpretation of the findings. He also argues that we assumed there would be 'one best way' to run a school. That is simply not so. As we stated in summarizing the findings:

> There is no one formula for success; what is needed will depend not only on the circumstances and history of each school but also on its particular aims and values. (Rutter, 1979)

Young further takes exception to our comments on the value of some degree of consistency throughout the school, and to our conclusions that

> it appears helpful for there to be some kind of consensus on how school life should be organized. (page 194)

His claim that we gave this an overriding priority is quite wrong, as readers of the book can easily see for themselves. His suggestion that our comments could be used as an excuse for heads to discipline dissident staff runs counter to the points immediately following those on consensus quoted above, namely

> For there to be an accepted set of norms which applies consistently throughout the school, it is necessary not only to have ways of ensuring that there is joint staff action but also that the staff feel part of a group whose values they share. (page 194)

Moreover the notion that we are proposing a suppression of differences of opinion is quite false. To quote again from the book:

> In view of the conflict between staff and pupils which, to some extent, is an inevitable part of schooling . . . joint activities outside the classroom may help each to appreciate the other better and come to share some of the same goals. (page 196)

or

> It seemed necessary that teachers should feel that they had some part in the decision-making process but also that they had sufficient confidence in the staff group as a whole that they were content for their opinions and suggestions to be expressed by someone else. (page 193)

or

> . . . uniformity of behaviour is unnecessary. Indeed, the greater the group agreement on crucial issues the greater the tolerance for individuality and idiosyncracy on other matters. (page 194)

In short, we agree with Young on the need to recognize and work through real differences. Conflicts of values and interests are inevitable in any organizational setting, and indeed the greater involvement of teachers in policy making in some of the more successful schools in our study meant that they were very much aware of differences between themselves and their colleagues. At none of the schools did all teachers agree completely on their objectives, but the more successful schools were those where some kind of working compromise had been reached between the demands of individual values and the needs of the organization. By contrast, the low morale of the less successful schools was much more likely to manifest itself in apathy than in conflict.

Research strategy and tactics

Several of our critics point to limitations of one kind or another in the procedures used to check whether the differences in pupil outcomes could be due, not to school influences, but rather to individual or family characteristics. Of course, there were very real limitations in the strategies and tactics we followed, as we tried to point out in the book, but the argument on possible school influences does not rest on one statistical procedure but rather on the combination of (a) showing that school variation was not explicable in terms of the intake measures used, and (b) showing that to an important extent it was explicable in terms of our school measures.

Thus, we deliberately chose a longitudinal strategy (necessitating a nine-year project) because we were aware of the crucial need to take into account the children's characteristics at the time they entered secondary school. None of the previous studies of schools had been able to provide any control for individual differences at the time of intake. Accordingly, the fact that we were able to control at all for intake variations was a major step forward. Of course, we were not able to have data on all potentially relevant intake characteristics. On the other hand, we did have data on the children's behaviour, non-verbal intelligence, reading, sex, socio-economic background and ethnicity. Previous studies have found these to be the most powerful predictive variables for the outcomes with which we were concerned. It is most unlikely that the addition of, for example, family size (as suggested by Tizard and Goldstein) would have substantially affected the findings. A comparison of various predictors of sixteen-year-olds' attainment in the NCDS cohort (Hutchinson *et al.*, 1979) confirms this conclusion, showing that family size makes only a very limited additional contribution to prediction when test scores at eleven-years-old have already been taken into account. Nevertheless, we agree (as we clearly spelled out in the book) that the fact that school differences remained after controlling for intake differences does not mean that the differences were due to school influences. That inference requires several other steps, the most important of which is the determination of whether the school differences were systematically associated with the characteristics of the schools themselves.

Here, we are criticized by Harvey Goldstein on the grounds that the school process findings could just as easily have arisen by chance, and that similar results could be obtained with purely random data. In fact, that is not so. There are three essential complementary strands in the argument. First, the number of statistically significant associations between the school process variables and the outcome measures far exceed those expected on the basis of chance alone. Second, the statistically significant associations were not randomly distributed; rather, they followed a pattern. Physical and administrative features were largely unrelated to outcomes, whereas features concerning the social organization of school life did show consistent relationships with our measures of the children's progress. Thirdly, other studies, using rather different research designs, have produced closely comparable findings in both of these respects. (As well as the studies cited in the book there are other investigations to which reference might be made — see e.g. Goldman, 1961; Pablant and Baxter, 1975; Edmonds, 1979; Lezotte and Passalacqua, 1978; Brophy, 1979; Brookover *et al.*, 1979; Pedersen *et al.*, 1978.) It is on that combination of steps that our argument on the probable importance of school process variables rests. However, as we make clear in the book, strong inferences on causation require the further step of the evaluation of planned change in schools (i.e. some form of 'experiment' which consitutes the essential sequel to epidemiological studies). Such investigations have yet to be undertaken, but they are much needed.

Statistical considerations

In taking up the specific points Goldstein raises on our methods of analysis, it should be emphasized that all methods of multivariate analysis have their limitations and their weaknesses, varying from one technique to another. In order to remedy one limitation all too frequently it is necessary to substitute another. Accordingly, the choice of method has to be made with proper attention to the particular characteristics of the sample and of the variables in each case. Not surprisingly, statisticians are not always in complete agreement on which method is most appropriate in any specific sample.

Nevertheless, in our own study, the main reason for using log linear methods of contingency table analysis was that many of the independent and the dependent variables were of a categorical nature. Some were essentially qualitative (e.g., sex or delinquency). Others, such as examinations or attendance, involved some implicit ordering but were not, perhaps, entirely satisfactory as ratio scales.

With data of this kind the log linear approach allows the inclusion of the desired variety of interactions in models of the observed cell counts. The procedure adopted was based on the following general lines. The variables fell into three sets consisting of outcome measures, school-based variables, and child-based variables. The selection of variables in each of the sets was guided by previous research findings. Clearly, the outcomes are related to the child-based variables, and schools differ in their composition of children. Furthermore, there are associations between variables within any of the sets. The analysis was then planned to answer questions of the following kind: Were outcome measures and school variables related in the presence of other interactions, or do school variables modify the relationship between child-based variables and outcome? As a consequence of the hierarchy of models, the latter question had to be answered first as clearly it subsumes the former.

This approach requires no assumptions about interval scales, linearity of correlation or homoscedasticity. The price paid is that there have to be rather arbitrary and fairly crude groupings. However, with the data to be analysed, this price is worth paying if the assumptions required in the more traditional correlational approaches cannot be met.

However, aware of the statistical differences of opinion on this issue, we also used linear regression analyses which, like the log linear modelling, showed a significant school process effect. We take the point about the relationship between the analyses in Tables 5.9 and 9.4 but an analysis along the lines suggested by Goldstein does not alter the finding that school process is still significantly related to outcome.

These issues are well known to researchers working in the field of study of possible school effects and it is regrettable that Goldstein dismisses our methods of analysis in disregard of both the issues and the fact that most statisticians working in this area now favour the approach we used. Our use of the G^2 statistic is also criticized as a means of comparing the relative importance of different variables — adding that these technical deficiencies 'do not encourage the reader to place a great deal of confidence in the authors' results'. His argument is based on the fact that the size of G^2 depends on sample size. Quite so, but of course in this instance we are using G^2 for comparative purposes only, within analyses in which the sample size remains constant.

Goldstein also comments on our use of significance tests but, within a single study in which the sample size remains constant, they do provide an indication of the relative importance of different variables at a given level of analysis. Thus, the fact that the school 'process' variables gave rise to statistically significant associations with outcome, whereas variables such as size of school or sex composition did not, means that within this sample of schools, school process variables were likely to be more important with respect to the outcome than the other variables studied. It was for these purposes only that we used statistical probabilities. Obviously, non-significant findings do not mean that the variables were of no educational importance even within the sample of twelve schools, and less so that they could not be of even greater importance in other samples of schools. The point is spelled out in the book (see pages 105 and 161) but he chose to ignore it. The only secure way to determine whether a relationship is actually important is to find out whether the same pattern recurs in other investigations. If it does, then, and only then, can one be sure that it is meaningful, although, of course, it may still be the result of systematic bias.

Jenny Hewison's point that our analyses do not quantify the magnitude of the school process effect in accounting for individual differences misses the point of our investigation. We were concerned with the question of differences *between schools* in over-all levels of attainment and behaviour, and not with the very different question of individual differences *between children.* It should be appreciated that schools may make a relatively small contribution to reducing variation between individuals but still make a major contribution to group levels of attainment or behaviour. The conceptual point is discussed by Jack Tizard (1975) with respect to the observation that over the last fifty years the average height of British school children has risen by 9cm, presumably as a result of better nutrition and better living standards. The rise in level, however, has had no impact on individual differences in height, where the population variance is largely attributable to genetic factors.

Policy and politics

Lastly, we need to consider the comments of both Tony Burgess and Michael Young on the policy and political implications of our work. Firstly, we should make clear that the study was not primarily 'policy research', nor was it intended to tackle political issues. Rather it was designed to study schools as environments for development. Of course, any investigation into schooling must be discussed in terms of possible policy implications, but our main concern was to describe current practice rather than argue a political case for the introduction of changes of any particular kind.

We regret that our focus on questions of social organization in schools has been taken to imply a gulf between our concerns, and those of the far larger number of writers who have explored issues of curriculum and pedagogy. Clearly these two sets of concerns are intimately related, and each demands the attention of the practitioner. We are in no sense suggesting that management is all, but we would nevertheless maintain that schools are managed institutions, and that research in this area can be of value to the practitioner. Clearly, it is possible to have a well-functioning school in terms of social organization which fails to develop effective and challenging teaching, but experience also suggests that in a school with low morale, or considerable disorder, the teacher attempting to introduce new approaches to learning is faced with very considerable difficulties. Both of these sets of issues — and the ways in which they interact with one another — need to be considered.

Having carefully thought about the points raised by our critics, we still hold to our conclusion that

> ... the results carry the strong implication that schools can do much to foster good behaviour and attainments, and that even in a disadvantaged area, schools can be a force for the good. (page 205)

We are only too well aware, however, that in answering some questions the study has either raised or emphasized others. To quote from our concluding chapter (pages 203-4):

> it is now important to go on to enquire how much (school) climates become established and then maintained or changed.

> We did not look in any detail at the particular styles of management and leadership which worked best; this is an issue which it is now important to investigate.

> An analysis of how classroom teaching is linked with school process factors as studied here would be rewarding.

and

> Finally, our study necessarily was concerned with correlations and associations. These suggest mechanisms and causal influences, but only studies of planned change in schools can identify these with any certainty. Such investigations are needed.

References

Brookover, W., Beady, C., Flood, P., Schweitzer, J. & Wisenbaker, J. (1980) *Schools Can Make a Difference* (in press).

Brophy, J.D. (1979) 'Advances in teacher effectiveness research.' *The Institute for Research on Teaching Occasional Paper No.18.* Michigan State University.

Edmonds, R.R. (1979) 'Some schools work and more can.' *Social Policy,* March/April 1979.

Goldman, N. (1961) 'A socio-psychological study of school vandalism' *Crime and Delinquency,* 7, 221-230.

Hutchinson, D., Prosser, H. & Wedge, P. (1979) 'The prediction of educational failure.' *Educational Studies,* 5, 73-82.

Lezotte, L.W. & Passalacqua, J. (1978) 'Individual school buildings *do* account for differences in measured pupil performance.' *The Institute for Research on Teaching Occasional Paper No.6.* Michigan State University.

Pablant, P. & Baxter, J.C. (1975) 'Environmental correlates of school vandalism.' *J. American Institute of Planners,* 241, 270-279.

Pedersen, E., Faucher, T.A. & Eaton, W.W. (1978) 'A new perspective on the effects of first-grade teachers on children's subsequent adult status.' *Harvard Educ. Review,* 49, 1-31.

Rutter, M. (1979) *Changing Youth in a Changing Society: patterns of adolescent disorder and development.* London: Nuffield Provincial Hospital Trust.

Tizard, J. (1975) 'Race and IQ : the limits of probability'. *New Behaviour,* 1, 6-9.